"Over the years I have read hundreds of books on church growth and church renewal. Most of the time I find there is one word that can describe them all…"tired." I confess I was a bit nervous when my friend Brian McMillan sent me his new book about the philosophy and ministry behind the growth of CenterPoint Church. I love Brian, but the last thing I needed was another "tired" book of solutions for dead churches. To my surprise, what I discovered was a book that can only be described as… "FRESH." This is not an already outdated book of "tired" ideas that once worked somewhere else for somebody else. This is a "fresh" word about what God is doing at CenterPoint Church, and what He wants to do everywhere in our day. I commend this book to you. Thank you Jesus for fresh strategies and thank you CenterPoint Church for sharing your journey."

DR. RON WALBORN, Academic Dean of Alliance Theological Seminary

"Brian McMillan and the staff at CenterPoint have been changing lives on Long Island for nearly a decade now, and I've been waiting a long time to gain this kind of behind-the-scenes access so I can steal some of their ideas!! This is a top shelf outfit with a back story that's really worth reading about. *Design* is a must-read for leaders, aspiring church planters and anyone interested in what God is doing on Long Island."

BERT CRABBE, Lead Pastor of True North Community Church, www.truenorthchurch.net

"This is not a 'how to' book on church growth, but the revealing of one pastor's heart's desire to know Christ and see as many people as possible discover the unmatched joy of surrendering our lives to him. Center-Point church has not grown by accident. Its growth is directly related to a strong vision, implemented with passion, and founded on a deep transparent love for Jesus Christ."

STEVE TOMLINSON, Senior pastor of Shelter Rock Church, www.shelterrockchurch.com

"Brian McMillian has been on a journey of sitting at the feet of Jesus and discerning the Master's heart. His life and ministry reflects the innovative heart of our Creator. Brian is especially gifted at practically applying what he is learning to the skill of leadership in the life of the church."

BRUCE TERPSTRA, District Super Intendant of the Metro Christian and Missionary Alliance, www.metrocma.org

"CenterPoint is at the forefront of ministry on Long Island and has been since their very first Sunday. Brian and his team set the pace on Long Island for aggressive church growth by reaching college students, young professionals, and young families with an informal and authentic approach to ministry."

CHRIS COATS, Associate Pastor of Creative Arts of Beacon Church, www.beaconchurchonline.com

Identifying God's
plan for His church

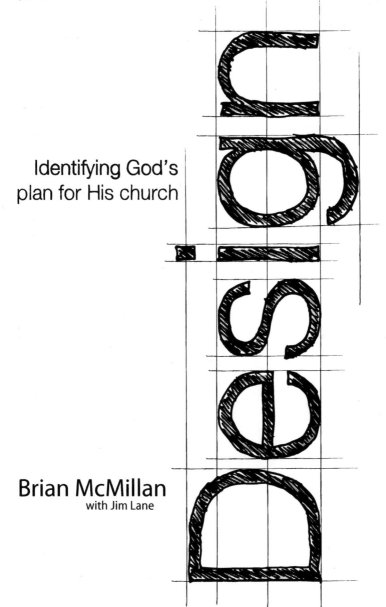

Brian McMillan
with Jim Lane

Edited by Nicole Jansezian.

Published by CenterPoint Publishing, publishing.cpchurch.com
2658 Corner Lane, Bellmore, NY 11710
www.cpchurch.com

Cover and book design by: Kirsten Doukas, pastelblack.net

Dedication

To my loving wife, Sarah.

I thank God for you everyday.

God brought you into my life at the perfect time and, without you, I wouldn't be the man that I have become today. And CenterPoint probably wouldn't have survived past year one!

Table of Contents

Introduction

Calling, Vision & the Journey

The thoughts in this book have been slowly developing for the last nine years. There has always been a clear calling on CenterPoint Church regarding our vision and direction, but to take vision from the conceptual stage and help it to come alive and become a living organism isn't easy.

For a church to be effective, I believe that its people must be sold out for Jesus, and have a thoughtful, *intentional* plan on how to reach people and help them to grow in Christ. Most churches have the heart, but they are missing the plan. They desire action, but they don't know which way to go.

Design is CenterPoint's account of how we are reaching people with the gospel. I have been writing this little book for more than three years in order to spell out the "what, why and how's" of CenterPoint. These pages capture our vision and our execution of that vision. The more a church's members and regular attendees know the ins and outs of their church, the more effective every ministry of the church becomes.

This book is also for other pastors and church leaders who are, like me, always wondering what makes other churches tick. I hope that this book will encourage you and help you on your journey as well.

Design is not the final authority on the ministry philosophy of CenterPoint. Just as it took many years for these ideas to come together, I'm convinced that a few years from now we will see some things differently and continue to adapt.

Part of our DNA as a church is to always be pushing ourselves to grow and explore what we can do to reach people for Jesus. We are a church of change. When a church stops changing, it quickly becomes stagnant—and life is too short to stay in one place.

I want to thank my dear friend Jim Lane for his help in getting this project completed. As I mentioned, I have been writing this book for a few years now. The problem has been that writing is not my strong suit. My "book" wasn't quite usable. As a result, I knew I needed someone to take some of my thoughts and bring clarity to them. So Jim's final responsibility as an associate pastor at CenterPoint was to spend a month translating some of my hieroglyphics into grammatically correct English. I want to note that Jim went beyond translating: He added many fresh ideas that helped to enhance each concept that is in *Design*.

I also want to thank everyone who has helped shape the vision of CenterPoint. Many of these concepts are not completely original, but gleaned in part from great church leaders across America who cared enough about other churches to write books and teach seminars.

Most of the ideas in *Design* are a result of rich conversations I've enjoyed with the leaders of CenterPoint who have been working tirelessly with me for the past nine years. It has been through much trial and error that we have come to a sweet spot in ministry and found our voice in the desert.

Lastly, I want to thank you for taking the time to read *Design*. My earnest prayer is that you will see yourself in this story, and for those who are part of CenterPoint, that your life will become its own chapter in the history of our church. Let us journey together as the body of Christ.

- BRIAN

Brian McMillan, Founder and Lead Pastor of CenterPoint Church

Part 1:

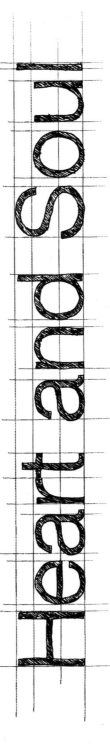

Heart and Soul

1: Seeing The Light

Sometimes it's tough to be a big-picture person. Day-to-day life is full of details demanding my attention, and this drives me bananas. I have found that the big picture and details are often mortal enemies for the human brain. At least mine. Every minute of every day tasks must be accomplished, items remembered, issues addressed, tweaked, messed with, noticed, or...forgotten. I find it hard to focus on details. So much so that even talking to you about it gives me the shakes!

Being someone who always sees the big picture means my mind is constantly steps ahead of reality. I wake up and see "future" in everything. Not necessarily *the* future as in a place in time, but characteristics of the future—*the potential*—of what

God could be doing and desires to do in, around and through us.

Yea, yea, I know you may be thinking that this isn't such a bad thing. And, I'll admit—I do like this about me. The problem, however, is when the big picture is superseded by all of those pesky details in my life. They bounce around in my mind like ping-pong balls in a cement room. It takes supernatural power for me just to focus in and grab one!

Over the years, God has helped me find a balance. He has helped me calm down and focus on the tasks at hand and to realize that working on details is critical if I ever plan on achieving the big picture.

The point that I'm getting at (if you're not stuck diagnosing my ADHD) is this: "What is the future?"

I don't consider myself a prophet or some kind of oracle—I can't see the future. Neither can you. However, we can see potential held within the future.

In you.

In me.

In His Bride, the Church.

It is here, in this outlook on the future, that our story begins. When I look at Long Island, I see a future laden with hope! I see a place populated by millions of people that God loves. And a place where God wants to make His name famous once again.

Here is what I long to see: The people here experiencing the love and grace of Jesus in such a powerful way that it changes the spiritual condition of Long Island. What an exciting thought! For a Christian, few things are more exhilarating than seeing God move in people's lives.

But then, I look at our society and reality puts a damper on my excitement. I can't even begin to imagine all the details that would be involved in arriving at the big picture. The work looks so difficult, the journey so long.

I have heard many Christians say that Long Island is spiritually oppressed. It would be hard for me to argue with that since the spiritual evidence is clearly visible. Just drive around on a Sunday morning: From town to town you'll see thousands of empty or near-empty church buildings, many of which are quite large and were filled to capacity when the Island flourished during vibrant seasons of faith. Then, churches struggled with where to put their growing congregations. But now, the ones that are actually still "open" on Sunday are considered fortunate. Most churches here plateaued decades ago, and have been in decline ever since.

Today, many churches have become virtual museums of what once was. They strive to preserve some long forgotten glory rather than impact the community for the Kingdom here and now.

The history of the church building in which CenterPoint meets is a great example of the state of the Church on Long Island. The prior church had a strong run of about eighty years of reaching and supporting the community. But it took just ten years and two new pastors to see its demise. Then the building sat as an empty reminder of a time when church, Christ and faith were once deeply visible in this part of New York.

The issue here isn't the number of people in the seats or on the membership roster. It's about churches effectively reaching their communities. It's about the very purpose of Church—God's people living for Jesus and showing His love to the world—being neglected. Whenever I drive by a church I wonder, what is its goal? What is its reason for existing? I wonder what its people are doing in God's name.

I realize that there are various reasons for a church's decline. Sometimes it is part of God's plan. When church leaders challenge their congregants more deeply or move the church in a new direction, attendance may decline as uncomfortable congregants seek easier living. Other times, a church may suffer from a population decrease in the area.

So I'm not tossing stones of blame through everyone's window. However, when the people of God make faith about man-made legacy and move away from the Gospel, things can go incredibly amiss.

Here is the simple point: Somewhere along the line "church" became about religion, and not about the Gospel. The institution of church took over as the purpose of church.

The funny thing about institutions is that they seem a lot like corporations. When I think of a corporation, I think of something cold, distant and self-serving. I think of someone who wants to sell me something, who wants to use me for their gain.

I believe the average person views church in the same light. Do you?

Religion, not Jesus or the Gospel, is one of the biggest deterrents to people experiencing the love, forgiveness and grace of God.

If churches continue to operate as institutions, out of their past momentum with no sense of how God is moving today and how He is drawing them toward the future, fewer and fewer people will come through their doors. The organic nature of how God works through His church will be lost. The once thriving spiritual heartbeat of a town will become barely an afterthought.

From what I've seen in the 15 years I have lived on Long Island, most of the four million souls living here have gotten only a small glimpse of God's truth. They haven't experienced that there is so much more to God's story.

Because religion can't capture the *heart*.

Year after year, Easter after Christmas, people leave church disappointed. Their spirits cry out, "This is the last time I give the church a chance to show me God." Another decline is seen in the pews. And, forget the pews—for these people, it's another year removed from a life-giving relationship with Jesus Christ.

This is truly heartbreaking for me. How can the most exciting, life-changing truth ever told end up as a boring, distant, irrelevant faith? Where did the light of the Gospel go?

BEING THE LIGHT

> *"In the beginning was the Word, and the Word was with God, and the Word was God. He was with God in the beginning. Through him all things were made; without him nothing was made that has been made. In him was life, and that life was the light of all mankind. The light shines in the darkness, and the darkness has not overcome it...Yet to all who did receive him, to those who believed in his name, he gave the right to become children of God—children born not of natural descent, nor of human decision or a husband's will, but*

born of God." (John 1:1-5, 12-13)

This is what drives me: the simple belief that Jesus is the answer. All human betterment comes when people put their faith in Christ and then reflect His light to the world.

This happens through a two-step process that takes a lifetime to develop. When we put our faith in Jesus and ask for forgiveness, we are made new. This is step one. Our past mistakes, which the Bible calls sin, are supernaturally washed away and we become children of God. As simplistic as this may seem, it is a real process for all of us.

The second step, however, is a whopper! This is when we start to live out our faith and we work! (Yep, there is work involved in following God.) We develop into people of love, compassion and action. We see our lives not as our own, but as God's. As we experience the love of God, it changes our perspective of life.

We are called to be the light of God in the world.

We are called to live and love like Christ did.

We are called to follow in His footsteps.

Doesn't this seem more like an adventure than religion?

Don't underestimate the power of what it means to be woven into God's story!

Even though thousands of churches are still operating

on Long Island, we believe God called us to start something new. We began as a church without the luxury of a past, but that made us willing to stretch ourselves each day. Instead of dwelling on the glory days of old, we live in the potential of the spiritual renewal of tomorrow.

It is hard for me to rest in the accomplishments of yesterday. And it is hard for me to sleep at night knowing that millions of Long Islanders still need to meet Jesus.

My prayer is that as you are reading this, you are also moved by this call!

This is the heart and purpose behind CenterPoint: We believe that the people of Long Island matter to God, and that His church is called to be the light that reveals His love. I pray that no matter where you live, that this is your heart for your city, state, and country as well. The rest of this book explains how we at CenterPoint execute this vision.

I've always been amazed at how God chose to share His redemptive plan with the world. He didn't engrave John 3:16 in the sky so that we would see it during every full moon. He didn't make the wind to sing the story of Jesus. No, God chose for His truth to be revealed through people who experience His love. His Church. That, by the way, is you and me.

The last words of Jesus were the beginning of it all:

"Then Jesus came to them and said, 'All authority in heaven and on earth has been given to me. Therefore go and make disciples of all nations, baptizing them in the name of the Father and of the Son and of the Holy Spirit, and teaching them to obey everything I have commanded you. And surely I am with you always, to the very end of the age.'" (Matthew 28:18)

This is why I love the Church: We get to play such an exciting part in God's redemptive plan for humanity. In word and deed, we are called to live out the message of God's love. What an awesome responsibility!

This book describes CenterPoint Church's effort to live out this message and calling from God.

Every church has the same calling, but the way in which they implement it will always be unique. Without a design, things fall apart. Without intentionality, nothing happens. So after much time and prayer, victories and failures, laughter and tears, and trial and error, we are honored to present to you God's design for CenterPoint Church.

2: Humble Beginnings

To understand the design at CenterPoint, you need to understand our story. It is in our humble beginnings that the plan began to unfold.

Our journey to becoming CenterPoint Church originated long before there was a building, a worship team or a mission statement. Its seeds began to take root in my heart when I was about twenty years old and leading a college and career ministry at a Baptist church in Wantagh, New York.

I was struggling with the conventionally accepted definitions of "church," and how God wants His people to worship Him and interact with their surrounding world. I was hit hard by this realization: In many churches, tradition had become the primary driving force of the "what, how and why" of their ministries. Sadly, this was at the cost of being relevant, healing and freeing to those who would come to Jesus for the first time.

I believed then, as I do now, that if Christians continued down that path, it would not be long before churches would become completely irrelevant. The Church risked—and risks—becoming frighteningly devoid of the presence of Christ Himself.

Tradition doesn't determine what we are called to do; *God* does. It is through a deep relationship with God that our steps as individuals and as a church are guided. *The past should be respected, but we live for the present and adapt for the future.*

After wrestling with all these thoughts about church for a couple of months, I began meeting and praying with four other friends about the pretty wild idea that God might be leading us to start something different on Long Island. By the summer of 2001 we were convinced that this indeed was something God was doing and announced to the college and career group that we were planting a church.

I shared the passion behind this future church, that it would adhere to accepted, historic Christian theology, but be free within that framework to look different in order to attract people. This church would not only make a difference in individuals, but also in the culture. Most importantly, it would be a church where all would be done for the glory of Christ and for His sake. At the end of the night, I extended an invitation to anyone in the group to join me if they were interested in sharing this journey of faith. It has been more than ten years since that night. I still remember wondering if I was really hearing from God.

Honestly, that might have been the most frightening night of my life as I stepped out further in faith than I ever had before, or since. I realized that I was opening myself up to scrutiny and possibly failure. I really wondered if any of the one hundred people that were in attendance that night would be foolish enough to join the five of us on this journey.

A few weeks later we had our first official "pre-launch" meeting at my parents' home in Massapequa, New York. My parents had just added a new family room onto their house, in large part so that we would have a place to meet. Now that's extreme parenting!

By the way, you should probably consider whether you are really ready to start a church if you are single, living at home and still mooching off of your parents. The situation can make for some strange conversations: "Hey mom and dad, can I have church in the living room next Sunday night? I promise we won't be too loud!"

Within six months, twenty-five people had decided to

join our little experiment. We met every other Sunday night to worship and pray together. We would spend hours in that living room being knit together by the Holy Spirit. Those six months are still the most precious church experience I have encountered—the glorious simplicity of it all! I have never felt closer to people and to God as I did in those days.

I sometimes wonder if we should have just stayed in the living room of my parents' house, meeting weekly and worshiping, not thinking about the next steps. Forgetting the design. Just doing church as we were. After all, home churches aren't the most far-off concept in Christendom. But that wasn't God's call for us. It would have been selfish of us to never leave the "mountain top" experience. Too much work needed to be done and this church wasn't, and still isn't, about us.

This reminds me of the transfiguration of Jesus, described in Matthew 17:1-5:

> *"After six days Jesus took with him Peter, James and John the brother of James, and led them up a high mountain by themselves. There he was transfigured before them. His face shone like the sun, and his clothes became as white as the light. Just then there appeared before them Moses and Elijah, talking with Jesus. Peter said to Jesus, 'Lord, it is good for us to be here. If you*

wish, I will put up three shelters—one for you, one for Moses and one for Elijah.' While he was still speaking, a bright cloud enveloped them, and a voice from the cloud said, 'This is my Son, whom I love; with him I am well pleased. Listen to him!'"

I think Peter was a New Yorker, always quick to share his thoughts and opinions. Rumor has it, in the most prestigious of theological circles, that Peter wore a Yankees hat and spoke with a Brooklyn accent. I'm just saying! But seriously, when Peter spoke, he usually *misspoke!* The transfiguration was the moment when God revealed the glory of Christ. The veil of His humanity was lifted and the three disciples closest to Jesus experienced the beautiful intimacy of witnessing the true power of the Kingdom of God in Christ. What a moment!

Ah, but then we have Peter. He saw all of this and blurted out the first thought that ran through his mind: "Let us build shelters!" Peter missed the bigger picture. He wanted to set up new meeting tents where God would once again speak to His people as He did when the Israelites were wandering in the wilderness. Peter must have thought, it can't get any better then this! The transfiguration, however, wasn't the fulfillment of Christ and it wasn't the end of the story. For the disciples it was a glimpse into *what is to come*—the King of Kings in all of His glory. But in order for this to happen, for Jesus to be manifest as king, He still had work to do. He still had a cross to bear. And so, they left the mountaintop because Jesus knew His life wasn't His own.

At every stage of our church's growth, I've heard people say that they miss the way it once was. We miss when we were twenty-five people and meeting in a home. We miss when we were seventy-five people or one hundred fifty people or two hundred fifty people. With each step of growth, I can honestly say I miss the previous stage as well. Each stage of growth has its own mountaintop experiences where everything just seems perfect and we would like to build our shelters and stay there awhile.

But as God's people, we are called to move forward. Church isn't about us, it's about us fulfilling God's design for us. And that does not involve staying on our mountaintop, but bringing the Creator of our mountaintop to the world.

3: And They're Off!

"But God chose the foolish things of the world to shame the wise." (1 Corinthians 1:27)

In those early days, we had no idea what to name our church. Choosing a name might have been the most difficult part of the process. At first, we were called No Greater Love Fellowship. We knew we had to change that after we became known simply as NGLF. The initials were odd enough, let alone people trying to come up with their own acronym, and not always appropriate ones at that. Okay, now stop trying to create your own! But if you come up with something really ingenious, email me!

On January 6, 2002, CenterPoint had our first official service at the Knights of Columbus (K.O.C.) Hall in Massapequa Park, New York. We had a sweet disco ball in the center of our "sanctuary" and the smell of stale beer from whatever party was held there the previous day. For those wanting to do church differently, this was instantly home. I was twenty-five at the time, still living at home and had just started dating my wife-to-be, Sarah. Only now can I admit this: CenterPoint wasn't the easiest church to take seriously!

The initial twenty-five people who comprised our church were all in their early to mid twenties. Well, except for my parents. Most new people thought my dad was the pastor, not his son who looked like a senior in high school.

Since we assumed we wouldn't reach any "real" adults anyway, we determined that our Sunday service should be at a most palatable time for our peers. We figured the people with whom we would connect would possibly be hung over on a Sunday and unable to attend church before noon. Our goal wasn't to reach Christians from other churches, rather those who had never entered one or who had long ago given up on church. We were trying to attract those from what we called the 3C's of Long Island: Clubs, Coffee houses and Campuses. These were our people! So we held our Sunday service at seven at night.

ONE DOWN

Our very first Sunday was amazing. We had 107 people show up! Standing room only. I felt like the rock star of church planting. I assumed that when everyone went home and told their friends about how great we were that the following week we would have to hold our service in a revival tent. The Nassau Coliseum was probably six months away, a year tops.

Then came week two. Let's just say it was a sobering night.

Some pastors like to play this game where, from the beginning of the service through worship, we don't look behind us to see the crowd. We let the people slowly file in. Then when it's time to teach, we walk to the podium, turn around and, *voila!* We see a full church. When I got up to teach that second night, I expected to see people sitting in the aisles, standing in the back and perhaps even one brave soul hanging from the disco ball. However, when I finally did turn around, what I actually saw were a mere forty-two people looking back at me. I know this was far from failure, but it brought me down to reality. There would be no Nassau Coliseum that year. Actual hard work was ahead of us. Getting this church to make a real impact would take more than just opening up our doors and expecting people to show up.

I couldn't admit this to myself until years later, but our

first few services resembled more of a middle school band recital than people looking to get plugged into a church body. Half of the congregants were parents who came to watch their kids "put on church." I quickly canceled my order for the revival tent.

Fortunately, things did start to improve from there. The rest of the year was marked by anticipation and growth. That founding group of twenty-five grew quickly to ninety consistent attendees by the end of the year.

Even though there was a lot to learn, and we were, in many ways, "rookies," we knew that our actions were marked by a passionate knowledge that we had been called by God to do this. We knew that God would be faithful to this call on our lives.

For all the things we lacked, the one thing that we had in abundance was a desire to bathe this church in prayer. That's pretty much all we did, week after week. We cried out to God on behalf of Long Island. We prayed for a miracle, and we prayed for a revival. When anyone asks me how we have been able to succeed as a church, I point back to these humble nights of passionate prayer. For any future church planters out there, please don't miss this—the primary responsibility of your team should be to seek God in prayer. Everything else you need to do is important, but all your efforts will fall short if prayer isn't the foundation.

Since we started, I've learned a lot about how to plant a

church, the different theories and statistics. This has convinced me of one simple truth about CenterPoint: It is a miracle that we didn't crash and burn that first year. We lacked everything you need to equip a start-up church. We had no money, no outside support, no experience and no education. Quite frankly, I really don't know what we were thinking. Well, that's not exactly true. We knew what God was calling us to do. We had faith in a big God and we had the desire to obey Him.

This applies to each of us, and our hope is that you recognize this truth for your own life: *God's call is often far beyond what we can wrap our minds around.* Many times we fail to see with the eternal perspective He has. He may call us to something far too big (or far too small) for us to comprehend, but to walk in faith and embrace that call means to trust His wisdom versus our own.

We didn't know specifically what kind of church we were becoming, where we were headed or what God was doing. But we knew we were being woven into a wild and awesome story.

I would say the same thing about you right now: You are being woven into a wild and awesome story!

4: Momentum

The year 2003 was marked by extraordinary momentum. By July we had outgrown the K.O.C. building and needed a larger location. We moved on to the American Legion hall in Seaford, a neighboring community on Long Island. It also featured a disco ball and the smell of stale beer, so we felt right at home.

After moving into the new building, it didn't take long before we needed to add a second Sunday service, which we set for eleven in the morning. The second service wasn't added due to lack of space at the evening one, rather because we had our first family attending the church. Little kids apparently go to bed before college students, who knew? I also had the premonition, amazingly, that as others in the church got married, perhaps that would lead to more babies. Yes, I realize, my skills of deduction are uncanny. Man+woman=babies. *Good thinking, Brian!* So we took that as a sign to step into unfamiliar territory, the "AM."

Starting a morning service was like starting a new church all over again. We would have a rocking PM service with about one hundred fifty people at night. But the early service was a very different story. The AM had about forty people in a room that held more than two hundred, and many of the tired attendees wished they could be transported to the PM service. The first year of the morning service was rough! Actually, I hated it. Every other Sunday I debated pulling the plug and going back to just a night service.

Nevertheless, God's faithfulness remained evident. It became clear that we were beginning to reach beyond the young adult age bracket into new demographics, including "thirty-somethings" and young families. Even some gray hair was showing up!

As the church continued emerging, we were overwhelmed with gratitude that God was helping us become a stable and influential place of worship and connection on Long Island. Some other pastors and churches even started to somewhat respect us. At least I hoped they did.

FINDING A STRIDE

When things happen quickly, it's hard to think of yourself as "finding a stride" because, often, you're barely keeping up yourself! However, in CenterPoint's case, those next three years had a pretty quick pace. It was something to the effect of, *"Buckle up and hang on! God is moving fast!"* We felt a palpable sense of velocity each week. Only a couple years before we were a small group of young adults jumping headlong into God's will. But now we had this church with adults of all ages and many children running around—everywhere.

Our vision continued to be refined and new ideas were implemented. The buzz of change and growth was constant. You cannot imagine the sense of pure joy and hope we felt when, on October 15, 2006, No Greater Love Fellowship became Center-Point Church, and we moved to our first actual church building, at 2658 Corner Lane in Bellmore!

BUILDING CHALLENGES

We had some challenges as we transitioned to the new building. It was old and in a state of disrepair. Its last church services were two years prior. The location was also less than ideal, being more than half a mile off of the last main street on the south shore, hidden in a residential neighborhood. Our location is pretty much the last place you'd look for a church. Any book on church growth would advise you to avoid this location. But as in so many areas of life, if we wait for the ideal, we wouldn't ever do anything. So we took on the challenge of moving into a dilapidated, hidden church building.

If we have anything at CenterPoint, we have hardworking, devoted and resilient people who put their sweat and energy into serving and getting things done. Since our location was less than ideal, our people worked hard to tell others about their church, even excitedly offering invitations to a place where they found the "living water" of which Jesus spoke in the Gospel of John.

The building needed a lot of work. We built additions and repaired the roof and ceiling. Walls were torn down and new ones were put up. And, by word of mouth, we continued to draw people from a variety of locations. Though we are not yet centrally located in Nassau County, we have been blessed with regular attendance and connections with folks from all over. Some come from one end of New York, the Bronx, while others from the other end, in Suffolk County. It's humbling to know that people are coming from great distances to worship with us.

As I write (and rewrite) this chapter, CenterPoint continues to move forward. We moved to our hidden building in October 2006 with an average Sunday attendance of one hundred ninety people. Now in 2011, more than five hundred attend on a Sunday and we have just added a fourth service. Not bad for a church that can't be found!

Yet as we look ahead to future building projects and prayerful and strategic planning, we realize that the next phase of our church means even more change. What brought us to this point won't be the same as what will get us to the next point. Without God's wisdom and direction, we are lost. As quickly as a church can grow, it can also decline. If the closest you ever come to CenterPoint is picking up and reading this book, we would be blessed by you taking just a moment to pray for us.

REFLECTING

As I look back to those early meetings in my parents' living room, I remember my fears, doubts and the bouts of anxiety. We wondered if we were actually doing God's will or not. I look back now and smile, and I thank God for giving us courage to jump so readily into the unknown.

It's an encouragement for anyone who is now a part of CenterPoint to look back at how our church began—with a handful of single, young adults—to reflect on what it has now become. We are thrilled to welcome you into this story.

Part 2:

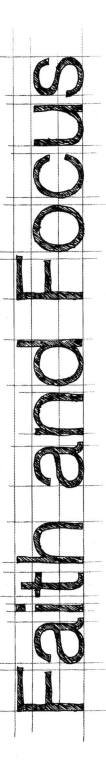

Faith and Focus

5: Vision

In 2003, CenterPoint Church's mission statement was developed:

> *"It is the vision of CenterPoint Church to be a community committed to bringing the Gospel of Jesus Christ and its power to Long Island. The church seeks to provide a loving, accepting atmosphere where the emerging culture can experience God through a life of worship. We believe God has called us to be ready to move when He leads, to be flexible in our structure and to embrace change. We long to see revival take place on Long Island and will seek to raise up leaders and plant churches according to His will and direction."*

It's always a challenge to write a mission statement. Describing your vision and setting your goals for the next few years in just a few words is stressful. Listening to what God is leading you into and writing it down is relatively simple, but developing a vision with quantifiable, meaningful and attainable goals is another thing altogether!

Of course, the work isn't over once you've developed a mission statement. It's only really just begun.

As we craft our ministry around the vision, questions continue to emerge upon which the elders and I (the governing body of church leaders) consistently reflect:

- What do we want to define us?
- What do we want to do really well?
- How can we make the greatest impact on Long Island?
- How are we going to reach our goal to plant churches and see revival here?

We must keep these things at the forefront of our thoughts. With so much happening these days, it would be easy to plug along without direction, just working on "getting things done." This is risky, because we can easily wind up off course. Just think of the times when:

- You're driving down the expressway and you look away for a second only to realize you missed your exit...and now you get to spend a bonus half hour in traffic!

- Between the demands of work, school, home and life, you realize it has been too long since you've spent meaningful time with your loved ones.

- You miss church here and there and before you know it, you're feeling loosely rooted at best, and fully disconnected or alienated at worst.

It's very much human nature to "plug along" in life and leave our direction undefined. Unless we stop and evaluate our life and direction, we can easily find ourselves coasting in an area with no real idea where we're going.

Left undefined, our direction will be determined by something or someone else.

So we need to regularly ask ourselves the above-mentioned questions about our direction, affections and decisions as a body. We'll begin to answer them here, as we show you how we hope to accomplish the vision of CenterPoint Church.

FOUNDATIONS

Through the big and the small, the seen and the subtle, there must be an intentional design to the way people embrace the life of a church, and, more importantly, their lives as Christians. In the coming chapter, we will examine the three foundational concepts that help us put "skin" on the design that we believe God has outlined for us to reach our culture:

- Christ First
- An 'Attractional/Missional' Ministry Approach
- A 'House' Concept

These big-picture principles for our church are years in the making. They reflect our hope to achieve a balanced ministry that will meet people's needs, enable them to be involved, encourage them to serve and allow them to get plugged into a caring community where healthy relationships will foster a more devoted walk with Jesus.

These foundations are interwoven and, when implemented properly, will form the most efficient means to reach our immediate community of Bellmore, the surrounding South Shore and, ultimately, all of Long Island as our members extend their own influence in their individual communities.

6: Christ First — It All Comes Down to Jesus

I have been to countless conferences and have read my share of books about how to grow a church. I have heard the theories, ideas and strategies and the many do's and don'ts. I believe that you must have a goal and be intentional if you want to see growth. However, unless you are in love with Jesus and fully dependent on the Holy Spirit, any and every structure or theory on church growth is pointless. This is woven into the vision and design of CenterPoint.

In fact, to keep us true to this, we consistently ask ourselves this question: "Is Jesus our mascot or our Messiah?"

Design

MASCOT VS. MESSIAH

When Jesus is your Messiah, He is at the center of everything you do. Part of the reasoning behind our choice of church name is that we deeply desire Jesus to be our centering point.

Churches can do all kinds of good things in the name of Jesus, even all of the things normally associated with church: worship, prayer, preaching, service—and still misplace Jesus entirely. It is in those instances that Jesus has become more of a mascot than Messiah.

At my high school in Fairview, Pennsylvania, our mascot was a tiger. Someone would dress up in a tiger outfit and stir up the crowds at pep rallies. We played the song "Eye of the Tiger" before football games and cheerleaders painted whiskers on their faces. The tiger wasn't simply the common theme of every event at Fairview, it was our identity.

A mascot brings continuity. It gives the organization a face and an idea to rally around as a sort of "branding" effort. The simple job of the mascot is to create an image through which people can unite. But in the end, all a mascot really does is put on an outfit and run around to get the fans excited. The tiger wasn't the reason students rooted for the team or the reason athletes tried to win their games. We didn't depend on the tiger for strength, wisdom or meaning in our lives.

Once we put our faith in Jesus, we find our new identity in Him. 2 Corinthians 5:17 says, *"Therefore, if anyone is in Christ, he is a new creation; the old has gone, the new has come!"*

We call ourselves "Christians" in order to represent this transformation in Christ. But in our effort to share the Gospel with the world, we've created thousands of Christian products and ideas. Christian T-shirts, video games, politics, diets, cruises and even mints (Test-a-mints. Sad, right?). In all this we run the risk of stripping away the deity of Jesus and making Him into a mascot.

It is as if we graduated from rooting for the Fairview Tigers to rooting for Team Jesus. You can almost hear the roar of the crowd as the pastor tosses the Hail Mary pass to the deacon for the touchdown and win. "Amazing Grace" begins to play and we all go out to the diner afterwards. You can't help but walk away from many churches and Christian events these days and get this sort of feeling—as if it's all a pep rally for ourselves, oh, and our mascot, Jesus!

Churches may sing about Jesus, read about Him and even hear about Him. The people may authentically like, or even love Him. But many times, Jesus is nowhere to be seen in the church. Somehow, in the business of preparing for the big game, we forgot to invite Jesus.

But Jesus should be the one holding the ball.

He's the only one saving the day. He's the only one for whom the crowd should be cheering, because it's all about Him in the first place. In case you haven't guessed yet, the point is this: We don't want to make CenterPoint Church famous. We want to do our part to continue to make the name of Jesus famous! He is our Messiah, not our mascot.

7: Being Christ-Driven, Not Self-Driven

"As Jesus and his disciples were on their way, he came to a village where a woman named Martha opened her home to him. She had a sister called Mary, who sat at the Lord's feet listening to what he said. But Martha was distracted by all the preparations that had to be made. She came to him and asked, 'Lord, don't you care that my sister has left me to do the work by myself? Tell her to help me!'

"'Martha, Martha,' the Lord answered, 'you are worried and upset about many things, but only one thing is needed. Mary has chosen what is better, and it will not be taken away from her.'" (Luke 10: 38–42)

I believe this story is a major challenge for every Christian and church. Martha is running around doing her best to make sure everything is perfect for Jesus. She's working hard and exerting herself and she gets angry when Mary doesn't do the same.

Mary, on the other hand, just wants to soak in Jesus' presence. She wants to sit at His feet and hang out with Him. To Mary, doing good works, serving and producing results is not as important as being with Jesus.

You know where we're going with this. More often than not, Christians act more like Martha than Mary. For CenterPoint to be a "Mary" church, we must, first and foremost, spend time in the presence of God, at the feet of Jesus, finding our satisfaction, fulfillment and identity there, dwelling in His presence.

Clearly this does not mean that we don't need to serve! God calls us to serve one another. But our focus must be in the right place. We want to be Christ-driven, not self-driven. Being Christ-driven needs to be the undercurrent of what we do and that comes from spending time in His presence.

God's Presence

So what was it that Mary enjoyed so much, basking in the presence of Jesus? Let's look to the book of Exodus to get a better idea:

"Moses said to the LORD, 'You have been telling me, "Lead these people," but you have not let me know whom you will send with me. You have said, "I know you by name and you have found favor with me." If you are pleased with me, teach me your ways so I may know you and continue to find favor with you. Remember that this nation is your people.'

"The LORD replied, 'My Presence will go with you, and I will give you rest.'

"Then Moses said to him, 'If your Presence does not go with us, do not send us up from here. How will anyone know that you are pleased with me and with your people unless you go with us? What else will distinguish me and your people from all the other people on the face of the earth?'

"And the LORD said to Moses, 'I will do the very thing you have asked, because I am pleased with you and I know you by name.'

"Then Moses said, 'Now show me your glory.'"

(Exodus 33:12-18)

Oh to have this sort of boldness today to ask, even demand, to see God's glory!

But do not miss this: God's presence reveals God's people. As His people, we should not want to do anything without His presence leading us or going with us.

What matters when we come together at CenterPoint Church is that:

- God is there.
- We sense His presence in our gatherings.
- He is pleased with our gatherings and our worship.

Material and temporary things like buildings and programs are merely tools He has given us for the work of the Kingdom. I have been keenly aware over the years that with all of the excitement about the building and the growth of emerging programs, that these things can become idols if they replace the priority of God's presence in all we do as a church.

If the end goal is spiritual transformation, God's presence must be the priority. It isn't really transformation without Him. So with that in mind we ask ourselves:

Are we praying?

Do we provide opportunities for prayer, and are people taking advantage of those opportunities? Is there a place for extended prayer in what we do? Are there prayer vigils? Are people praying before, after and during services?

Are we worshiping?

This is not about the method, but the heart of worship. We are not asking if people sing, we are asking if they worship. Do people connect with God during worship services? Are we walking people toward a lifestyle of worship? Here is a real big clue: If it seems more like a concert or karaoke, there's a strong chance that it isn't worship.

And finally, are people being transformed?

Are people seeking God's fingerprints on their hearts and lives? Are they desiring that their minds be renewed? Are people seeking a Romans 12:1 lifestyle, to *"offer your bodies as living sacrifices, holy and pleasing to God—this is your spiritual act of worship"*?

A life devoted to Jesus includes internalizing God's Word, fellowship, compassion for and service to those in need, living a life of holiness, and so on. But a good starting point for all of this is to continuously strive to be in God's presence and let that overflow into the rest of our lives.

If people seek God honestly, God is faithful to guide them appropriately.

As a result of dwelling in His presence, churches are released to move toward whatever ministry model God is leading them, whether based on programs or small groups, purpose-driven or seeker-friendly, missional or traditional, contemporary or liturgical.

Each of these models has its pros and cons and each resonates differently with certain people. That is why God allows His Church to be so diverse in the first place. But only in His presence will you know which one is right for you.

At the end of the day, what matters is that a church is earnestly seeking God's presence and His call, not its own ministry preferences and personal comfort.

Part 3:

From Concept to Blueprints

8: An Attractional/Missional Approach to Ministry

Every church follows some sort of ministry model. Even if they've never explicitly decided to adopt one, they most likely fall into one of the categories we mentioned in the last chapter. Two of the models that are most often discussed in church circles these days are the "Attractional" and "Missional" models. To understand how these models influence CenterPoint, let's examine each one.

THE ATTRACTIONAL CHURCH

An attractional church is one built on the premise that it must draw unchurched people into its building in order to show them Christ.

For most attractional churches, Sunday is *the* day of the

week. It provides easily identifiable markers of whether or not the church's efforts in drawing people were successful: How many seats were occupied? How many people came to classes or programs? Did folks raise their hands during worship? How much money was in the offering?

In the attractional model, Sunday services affect everything the church does, including the way it attempts to reach people for Christ. Comfortable seating, snazzy video clips, modern worship music and even the building are used as evangelistic tools (the "Build-it-and-they-will-come" concept). Everything is designed to make Sunday shine and reinforce the aforementioned markers of success.

Nothing is inherently wrong with many of these goals as long as the purpose remains getting people connected to God on a deep and sincere level. In an attractional church, most of the effort goes into Sunday morning and, as a result, what you do on Sunday is the spiritual starting point of your entire ministry. Sunday is where "ministry" gets done and Sunday determines a church's success or failure.

There are a few shortcomings with this approach. Even though some people may come when asked to check out a church service or program, many more simply don't see the need to darken the doorways of a church no matter how "attractional" it is!

The pastor's wittiest series, the most comfortable chairs, the hippest worship and even the freshest coffee don't matter. Not to mention that an hour and half a week doesn't create a mature Christian. By itself, "attractional" just doesn't cut it.

THE MISSIONAL CHURCH

Missional churches, on the other hand, focus on bringing the church to the people rather than bringing people to the church. Take a look at this excerpt from The Shaping of Things to Come by Michael Frost and Alan Hirsch:

> "Historically the church has defined itself in institutional terms. That is, church leaders as well as Christians in general have regarded the church as an institution **to which outsiders must come** [emphasis ours] in order to receive a certain product, namely, the Gospel and all its associated benefits. In our view, the church should be missional rather than institutional. The church should define itself in terms of its mission— to take the Gospel to and incarnate the Gospel within a specific cultural context."

The institutional church over the years has sent a message to outsiders that goes something like this: "Hey you! Yes, you over there. Stop what you're doing, rearrange your life and come see what we have

69

to offer. If you want to hear our message of good news for your life, you are going to have to make some sacrifices, especially whatever you've got going on Sunday morning."

A missional church endeavors to change that message and take the church into people's lives, wherever they may be.

Here are some basic contrasts between attractional and missional churches:

ATTRACTIONAL	MISSIONAL
• Draw the people in	• Go to the people
• Get people involved in our world	• Be involved in the world
• Focus on Sunday	• Focus on Monday through Sunday
• Minister mainly in the church	• Minister mainly outside the church

When you start thinking missionally, you capture the heart of Christ and His mission for the Church. You bring the light of Jesus with you into the world, into the culture.

CENTERPOINT'S "ATTRACTIONAL/MISSIONAL" APPROACH

In a balanced form, both the attractional and missional approaches have benefits. Our approach is a hybrid of the two.

We simply—and not so creatively—call it an "Attractional/Missional" approach to church. This is a fundamental answer to what, how and why we do what we do as we attempt to reach people for Christ.

In order to understand how we apply our dualistic approach, let's look at our plan to excel in each of these areas.

9: The Best Stinking Attractional Church Around

We just read that in an attractional church, Sunday services are the big focus and are an important place to share the truth of Christ, but that we should avoid taking the focus on Sunday to extremes. Proponents of the missional approach also have great ideas, but they can become unbalanced and pessimistic in their opposition to Sunday's place in God's church.

At CenterPoint, we hold Sunday morning in higher regard than advocates of a purely missional model. The reason we believe our Sunday worship services are important can be seen in a passage from the book, *A New Kind Of Christian*. The author, Brian McLaren (*not* the Lead Pastor of CenterPoint, Brian *McMillan*), explains his *missional* approach in the following excerpt, but we think it actually supports our idea of a balance between missional and attractional approaches.

McLaren's book follows a pastor named Dan who is trying to find Christianity's place in today's culture. His journey leads him to a high school science teacher, Neo. Through a series of discussions, Pastor Dan starts to view church and Christianity in a new light. In this section, we read an email exchange between Neo and someone trying to come to terms with their faith in modern times:

> "COLBY: My name is Colby, and I'm a senior in computer science, although I've been thinking about going to seminary. Neo, I find it hard to believe that modern evangelical Christianity, of which I am glad to be part, is dying, as you suggest. I mean, aren't evangelicals the fastest-growing segment of the church? Look at all our Christian colleges and radio stations and TV programs and seminaries. I think you're a little premature in writing an obituary for modern Christianity. It looks alive and well to me.
>
> NEO: I would agree that the contemporary church is rich, somewhat powerful (though that's waning), and outwardly successful in many ways. And I would agree

that the evangelical church is the fastest-growing sector of the church at large, especially the charismatic wing, both domestically and globally. But that simply means that it has more to offer than the alternatives, which may not be saying much. It may also mean that the church is growing fastest where premodern people are coming to terms with modernity, and so the modern version of the faith offered by conservative Christianity is more up-to-date than their own medieval worldview. Remember, Colby, the whole world doesn't progress at the same pace, and in many places in the world, people still live in a medieval or even ancient and in a few cases prehistoric mind-set. Just because people perceive something is a step up from what they already have does not mean that it is the final step, the top step.

But also remember-the medieval church was never more powerful, large, rich or outwardly successful than it was around 1500. And dinosaurs were never more big and powerful and dominant than they were at the end of the Jurassic period. Think of it like this: if it were 1910, what kind of transportation would you buy? What would be the most reliable form of transportation available to you in 1910?

COLBY: I guess it would have been the automobile. It had been invented not long before that, right?

NEO: If you were looking for a good stock invest-ment, Colby, I'd wholeheartedly agree: the Ford Motor Company would have been a great investment. You're right—automobiles had been invented only a decade or two before. But in 1910, they were still notoriously undependable. Not only that, there weren't good roads for them to ride on, and there weren't any gas stations around. So if you needed good, reliable transportation, you would not have bought a car in 1910. What about airplanes? They were still seen pretty much as a joke, an impractical dreamer's machine-it had only been a few short years since the first one got off the ground. So if you wanted good, reliable transportation in 1910, you would have bought a horse and buggy. Why, never in history had better buggies been built! Do you see the point? We would expect that the best modern churches in history would exist today, right at the time when the modern world is passing, much like the world of the horse and buggy in 1910. The smartest modern churches see this and are building in flexibility so that they can "convert" to postmodern effectiveness in the future—perhaps like a foresighted buggy manufacturer who realizes he's not just in the buggy business but rather in the transportation business. He would continue building fine buggies but would be preparing to build automobiles too."

What we gleaned from this is that culture, like technology, is continually evolving, we don't know exactly what it is evolving into, and, moreover, we do not know what will be left behind from the previous era after the evolution is complete.

So, the almost obsolete form of transportation is still useful and is going to drive someone into a collision course with the God of the universe. But the new and upcoming mode of transport is still needed to drive others to their destiny with Him. In other words, we think it is the perfect time to build both buggies and automobiles.

We believe that people need Sunday:

For teaching

This gives the church an opportunity to hear a Biblical message that challenges the congregation to know God, understand sin and become a disciple of Christ.

For worship

Something supernatural happens when God's people gather together at a specific place and time to worship and adore Him.

For fellowship

People need to be able to interact and relate with those whom they share this good news, and a church provides a place of acceptance and safety in which these relationships can develop.

For evangelism

People are still giving their hearts to Christ, plugging into ministry and ministered to on Sunday.

For rescue

A church must reach out to, encourage, strengthen and rescue Christians who are wounded or whose walk with God may have broken down or become disoriented.

For vision

For the fifty-two Sundays of the year, prayerful and intentional teaching leads the entire church body on the same path, keeping the people united.

We'll delve more deeply into the attractional church attributes in which we want to excel, particularly involving Sunday, in the "Front Door" section of Chapter 12.

10: Keeping Growth in Perspective

Growth, for many churches, is the goal, the trophy, the prize. Churches around the world pray for "just one to be reached in the name of Jesus," and they throw innumerable resources into this single goal.

We believe deeply in and strive for growth. However, there is a huge difference between growing a church and reaching the lost. Unfortunately, the line sometimes gets blurred. I'm at a point where I avoid using the phrase "I want our church to grow," because it may imply the wrong goal. We don't want to simply grow, we want to lead people to Jesus.

Usually, when a church wants to focus on growth, it first targets the flavor of its Sunday service. In the last few decades, that has meant becoming more "contemporary." Churches get rid of their organs and the intimidating pulpit. They cut the choir, remove the pews and add cushioned chairs. Then maybe they add drums, guitar and video projectors to their services.

When churches attempt to "grow," they make sure they have cool music, a cool preacher, use pop culture references and, of course, serve coffee. They get out the message that things are different and that this is a place where people can "find what they are looking for" in a church.

We're not saying anything is wrong with this—after all, this sounds a lot like us at CenterPoint. I'm proud of who we are and that some consider what we do "cool" or relevant enough to bring their friends. Many of us who were raised as Christians have been embarrassed after inviting someone to a church, not because they were ashamed of the Gospel, but because of the disconnect between their church and the culture.

As a church starts to grow, it normally reaches people at three places of faith:

- Christians that other churches don't or can't reach, who have been marginalized or are "homeless" when it comes to church.
- People who were attending one church until they visited another one that they liked much better. Pastors of growing

churches don't like to talk about this group, because they've "hopped." *Many of you reading this as you drink your Iced Mocha Frappuccino have just realized we are talking about you! Don't panic—it's not necessarily a bad thing!*

- And the crown jewel of church growth: New Christians. This is truly a joy and is a real marker of growth. The problem is, this isn't a big percentage of the pie. Far from it!

Many reasons for leaving a church are well-founded, from unhealthy or overbearing leadership to twisted theology or a lack of progress. There is a time to stay and a time to move on. Growth based on "transfer" (or church hoppers), however, doesn't count as an addition to the Kingdom of God. Church growth should be based on people coming to know Jesus. We want to make sure this is the case at CenterPoint.

This is a call to all pastors: Don't celebrate if your church is growing. Celebrate if the Kingdom of God is expanding!

I believe that more churches with an "updated" approach are desperately needed. We don't want to lose people due to a lack of cultural relevance. So new churches, like ours, emerge. I love how our church looks, acts and sounds. We decided to do church with a modern flair because we desired something that matched the cry of our heart before God. And we were frustrated at watching our peers give up on it.

11: Missional Possible

For as often as I may use them, Christian buzzwords annoy me. I actually have tried to avoid using the word, "missional." The problem is, I haven't come up with a better word for it. Being missional is a topic that I teach on quite often and I just couldn't avoid using it in writing this book. But no matter what we call it, we need it. Without at least some form of missional living, the impact of our Christian walk is severely limited.

MAINTAINING A BALANCED MESSAGE

With roughly fifty dedicated members, CenterPoint had a strong missional vein running through its core in its first year. Our people lived for the sake of the Kingdom. They brought the message, joy, excitement and momentum with them wherever they went. They were Christians beyond Sunday.

Once Sunday attendance hit an average of a hundred people each week, we were encouraged: "We made it! This might actually work." Seeing growth can be addictive and so we began to desire more expansion, which isn't a problem until it becomes your focus. Growth as an organization is radically different than the growth of people. As our growth continued, Sunday morning services increasingly became the main ingredient of the church. By five years old, CenterPoint had become almost completely attractional, and we had lost our missional roots.

So we had to make the very intentional effort of regressing to the way things were. To teach, train and practice a missional lifestyle. Our belief has always been that individuals must grasp a missional lifestyle for themselves first in order for it to become the heartbeat of the church, even if we weren't always practicing it.

KEEPING A FINGER ON THE PULSE

How a church spends its time and money can be a gauge of how it balances attractional and missional ministries. How much is being invested in Sunday? How much is being invested in the rest of the week? How much is invested in programs? How much is invested in outreaches?

We periodically must remind ourselves of the main points of missional living:

- "Church" happens Monday through Sunday, not just Sunday.
- Real ministry is determined by how we impact others, not by our titles.
- We are to live holy lives for Christ in front of an unholy world.
- We reach out together through strategically created "missional communities."

Attendance on Sunday is far from the only marker of a church's health. The conventional church, in its establishment over the millennia, wasn't designed to function missionally, at least not for long. It was designed to maximize numeric growth on Sunday and, hopefully, foster an environment of spiritual growth.

Again, nothing is wrong with numeric growth as long as spiritual maturity and missional living remain at the forefront of our efforts. But it is something to constantly keep in prayer, don't you think?

You Need One Thing

We all know that no matter how good a sermon is, it rarely has the power to change someone's life. Sure there are moments when the Holy Spirit uses one special message to transform your life, but how many messages have you heard and really left as a new person? Simply hearing propositional truth isn't very effective at making us adopt it as truth in our own lives. Imagine how different life would be if we just did what we were told. Here are some familiar examples of what I mean:

> Parent: *"Drugs are bad for you!"*
> Child: *"Okay, I won't do them."*

> Mom: *"Your value isn't determined by whether a boy likes you or not."*
> Girl: *"Mom, you are so right."*

> Nutritionist: *"Eating healthy and exercising regularly is good for you."*
> Us: *"We're on it!"*

> God: *"You can eat anything else in the garden, but eating this one thing is a really bad idea."*

Adam & Eve: *"No problem, Lord, we won't."*

Alas, no.

We all need something more deliberate and a lot more concrete that just words in order for transformation to take root. No matter how much we preach "bring the church to others" and "become present in the world while not being part of it," you must desire this for yourself. And how does that happen?

I can see your minds churning now: *"It is a challenge to become a 'missional' person. Where do I begin? How can I, of all people, impact the community? What drives the missional person and church?"*

You need just one thing.

It is hard to attain.

It is spoken about, taught and prayed for a good deal.

Some assume they have it, and are wrong.

Others assume they don't have it, but they do.

Simply put—you must have an intense love for Jesus and a strong desire to live for Him so that, even when no one is looking, you do all for His glory and honor.

Yeah. Simple.

But this one thing affects everything about you, everything you do and your ability to walk missionally. To the extent that you have attained this love, you will walk missionally.

Honestly, it is a lifelong endeavor to live for Christ. We are broken people in a broken world and we are learning this walk daily. None of us have "arrived," and we know this. Not you, not church leadership, not even your Great Aunt Bonnie, the super-Christian matriarch in your family who smelled of lilacs.

LETTING GO

So since this is a level playing ground, let us take time out to reflect and ask ourselves a few questions. These are questions I ask myself as well:

- Knowing that repetition breeds habit, what am I willing to start doing consistently that would enable me to bring Christ to the world?

- Can I make "sacred space" for God in my day-to-day life? Can I journal, pray, meditate, study, be silent, find solitude and worship, not for the sake of accomplishment, but for the sake of relationship? Can I do these things to ensure a focus on missional living?

- With whom can I share my spiritual development? Is there a person who could act as my spiritual mentor? Is God leading me to mentor someone else? And that scary question: Is there someone who can hold me "accountable?"

- In what ways do I tend to make everything about me? How can I back away from this type of lifestyle and attitude?

When we read these questions, we realize there is a lot of *letting go* involved. We must release our intense grip on certain things we hold dear—time, comfort and control being just a few of them.

To live missionally is to back away from the compass of self that so permeates Christian society. Our home life, work life, play life and our Sundays must shift. We must rearrange the price tags on what we hold valuable and shift our thinking from, "how can I be blessed?" to, "how can I bless others?"

And when that shift takes place, we are ready to bring the Church to the world.

STEPPING OUT

One day, I realized just how trapped I was in the Christian bubble. I was challenging the leaders at CenterPoint to think about how they were living missionally. I intended to give some practical examples from my life, but found myself speechless—I realized I wasn't connected to anyone or anything outside of church! Among our leadership team, most of us spent all of our time with each other or at church. Somehow, in the midst of teaching people how to live like Christ, I had failed to live like Him. Jesus didn't hang out only in the temple, he visited the homes of sinners, people who would never step into a "church."

Yet I didn't know a single person who wasn't somehow part of a church. Pastors, if the only people we know are ones who attend our church we have a problem. We should know the people in the communities that surround our churches. They should know us because of our involvement in their lives and not because our name is on the church sign.

It was around this time that I started to make some changes in my own life and at CenterPoint. I become involved with the Bellmore Chamber of Commerce. I started up relationships with people in my town. I began to see the people of Bellmore as my church, they just didn't know it yet.

As for CenterPoint, we sponsored the town Christmas celebration and became active in the local street fair. We hosted a health fair and created a "GetFit Bellmore" forty-day health campaign that included free seminars.

Now, our community knows who we are. We are a part of their lives. They know we are here to serve them, even if they have never entered our church.

Many of our churches need to pop the Christian bubble that hides us from the community. We need to look for ways to serve and be involved with the people around us.

Design

If we don't serve our towns and show them we care, then why should they trust our message?

Missional churches must reexamine themselves. Why join the Christian softball league? Instead, join the local town league. Start a Boy Scout or Cub Scout troop instead of a Christian version that the neighborhood kids won't join. Have your Vacation Bible School target the community and not just your church.

There are so many opportunities for a church to be part of its community. Just read your local paper and you will find them.

93

12: House Concept

The "House Concept" is what we call the process people go through to become part of CenterPoint. From their first visit to the moment of partnership, we've recognized three steps toward becoming a committed part of our body.

It's kind of like moving into a house: You enter through the *front door,* you hang out in the *living room,* and eventually you *move in.* So we got really creative and entitled this concept the "House Concept," and came up with titles for each of these steps, or experiences:

- Front Door
- Living Room
- Moving In

THE FRONT DOOR

Now that we have filled your head with all things missional, it's time for us to come back to the attractional side of CenterPoint. We believe the "front door" experience is very important. We are intentional about it, trying hard to consistently look at the church experience through the eyes of first-time visitors. In this way we can try to make their experience a positive one and more effectively pave the way for relationships to develop.

The Definition

The front door is any of the first opportunities Center-Point and her people have to make a connection with others. It is first contact, the first impression and the first moments of interaction.

The church website is a great example of a front door. Imagine if someone sitting at home on a Saturday evening is searching the web for a church to attend tomorrow—and they happen upon our sweet site!

Another important front door is Sunday, when people come and visit our worship services. A front door could also be one of our C.I. (Common Interest) Groups where people get together and enjoy similar interests or hobbies. Or perhaps it is Vacation Bible School.

You get the point. These are first opportunities. And we refuse to underestimate their value. By ensuring our front door is open, we lay the ground work for relationship. This is a critical element as we walk with people on their way to becoming believers.

An 'Open' Front Door

What good is a door if it doesn't open? A front door should be obvious, free of clutter and easy to open even if you are carrying groceries and kids. The same is true with a church.

The best way for me to explain an open front door is to give some examples of a closed one. Some may sound familiar. Closed front doors exist when churches, programs or individuals, subtly or overtly, make a first connection with a guest awkward, frustrating, disappointing or even hurtful. For instance:

- A poorly designed website that is difficult to navigate and never updated.
- People in cliques that don't greet anyone outside their circle of friends.
- The greeters are grumpy, impersonal or simply nonexistent.
- Events or programs are poorly organized or self-focused.
- Church practices, language or sermons that seem 'normal'

to people raised in a church, but are completely irrelevant and confusing to newcomers.

On the other hand, open front door ministries make the most of every opportunity:

- They have a website that is welcoming, informative and easy to use.
- Church members and leaders take the time to genuinely engage with newcomers.
- Programs and events respect visitors with good organization and an accommodating, serving and giving attitude.
- Messages are relevant and engaging to everyone sitting in the service.

When we've accomplished this we open our front door wide and maximize opportunities:

- to meet people where they are
- to make people feel welcome
- to make inroads to relationship
- to take first steps toward sharing the Gospel of Jesus Christ

The front door exists for the newcomers as much as it does for current members.

We believe the Gospel of Jesus Christ is the greatest truth ever told and, since we are called to carry this great news to the world, we believe that we should treat every opportunity as sacred. We will go the extra mile to ensure that the people feel welcomed and safe and that their first interactions are fluid and meaningful. This "open door" concept overlaps with being attractional, and therefore is played out more so on Sunday.

HANDLING SUNDAY, THE BIGGEST FRONT DOOR

We treat Sunday as a time to introduce people to Jesus, as well as spiritually build up our community and celebrate God's love through worship. Let me say upfront, I realize the tension in this.

Americans understand that "church" happens on Sunday. Even if someone doesn't know anything about the Christian world, it is highly likely that if he or she wanted to get connected to a church, they would look for a Sunday morning service. This is why we consider Sunday to be CenterPoint's biggest front door.

Being the biggest entry point into our church, Sunday brings diverse visitors such as:

• The person who has never entered a church and knows nothing about Jesus.

• The person who grew up in church, but walked away.

• The person who was deeply wounded by a church.

• The Christian who is looking for a new church home.

The comfort zones of all of these newcomers' will vary. So we must ensure that not only is our front door open, but we try to avoid or mitigate practices that alienate, confuse or frustrate CenterPoint's new guests. The best way of accomplishing this is by examining everything we do through the eyes of people at every stage of their faith.

Ensuring Sunday is Open

You would be surprised at the number of subtle and not-so-subtle things that impact guests from décor to worship music to "lingo" or the way Sunday's message is presented even to the way that chairs are arranged.

The challenge is to ensure that we remain faithful to proper Christian doctrine while recognizing the church practices that aren't biblical and can be adjusted or removed. We realize that people come to church with all sorts of preconceived notions, but we want to create an environment where they feel safe enough to take down some walls and hear the true message of Jesus.

Here are some of the aspects on which we focused to make our Sundays open:

Vernacular or Christian 'Lingo'
We've struggled, even as we've written this book, because,

often when talking about God or Christianity, we tend to overuse certain words. When gathering on Sunday, it is important to back off the "Christian-ese" because new people may feel alienated by words that we as Christians take for granted. This is why whoever teaches at CenterPoint will define terms like saved, born again, sanctified, sin, salvation, etc. *We don't avoid these words, we teach them.*

I have been asked numerous times by people who are not familiar with CenterPoint if we are one of those "born-again churches." I'm sure they ask because they've had a bad experience with a "born-again Christian" who bashed them over the head with their Bible or a self-righteous attitude. To them, "born again" is to be avoided at all costs.

Knowing the cultural stigma of the term, each time I mention in a sermon that we are to be born again I explain that this is the spiritual process of being made new in Christ for *every* Christian in any denomination. The words came from Jesus Himself in John chapter 3:3 when he told Nicodemus, *"I tell you the truth, no one can see the kingdom of God unless he is born again."*

But for me to flippantly use the term on a Sunday would alienate many newcomers. I even regularly define the word "Christian," since many in our culture think that simply means being raised in a church.

Teaching (From the Stage)

Both newcomers and "veteran" Christians come from different backgrounds and experiences. CenterPoint is a melting pot of many faith and non-believing backgrounds. With all these different lives intersecting in one place, it is inevitable that some topics will draw strong emotional reactions from different people. For instance, the words, "Spirit-filled," will conjure widely divergent definitions and expectations for people from different church backgrounds. It is rare that everyone in a room would have the same theological "starting point." So our teachers are challenged to present material in a way that it can be received correctly and uniformly. Every week, in every message, we try to make our points as clear as possible to everyone.

Here is a dramatic real-life illustration of a message being skewed by nuances:

The Poisonwood Bible, is a book about a missionary named Nathan Price who headed to the Congo with his wife and children to preach Christ to the area's inhabitants. The mission in the Congo is very difficult, and Nathan is sorely unprepared. Lingala, the language spoken in that region, though beautiful, is extremely difficult to master. Words have wildly divergent meanings, though they sound very similar. The slightest change of intonation or inflection makes two seemingly similar words take on entirely new meanings.

You can see where this is going. Nathan, over and over, tries to declare to the tribe that Jesus is a very good thing and that He loves them, but instead communicates to the group that Jesus is like the poisonwood tree, which natives are afraid of and avoid, because they know that contact with it can cause a lot of pain, and can even kill them.

Clearly, here at CenterPoint, the "language barrier" is not as problematic. But we too must pay attention to who is sitting in our service on a Sunday morning and dropping their kids off in the nursery if we want the message to come across properly.

Handling Sensitive or "Hot Button" Issues

One of the challenges we have is to speak God's truth without beating people up with it. At CenterPoint, we try to deal with sensitive issues by not compromising the truth of God's Word, while exhibiting the grace, mercy and the compassion of Jesus.

Some churches are afraid of being soft on sin so they become heavy-handed and downright judgmental. On the flip side, other churches are fearful of being too judgmental and end up watering down or even ignoring God's stance on sin. For us, grace and truth go hand in hand. We never avoid calling sin what it is and challenging our people to be holy, but we do it as fellow sinners, struggling together as we flesh out our faith. It is a hard balance to find, but we work constantly to find it and pray we accomplish this.

You've heard it said a thousand times: "Love the sinner and hate the sin." We must recognize that when we "love the sinner," we are loving someone like ourselves. We are all sinners in need of a Savior.

I don't think that people mind being challenged as long as they know that the challenger sees his own imperfections and struggles, has compassion and walks with them, not ahead of them.

Pulling It Together

These practices are a large part of what makes our Sunday services attractional. Because of our consistency in our approach to Sunday, the people of CenterPoint feel comfortable and free to invite their unbelieving friends and family to church. If people don't bring anyone to church, we don't grow and neither does the Kingdom of God.

It is here that we see the missional-attractional paradigm come together. As we live missionally, we bring Christ to those in our lives. We serve them, help them, live with them and share with them the gospel. Sometimes we have the amazing privilege of walking them through the moment of realizing that Christ loves and forgives them. Or we plant the seed of truth into their lives that helps make faith in Christ tangible to them. Or, we invite our friends to church, and it is here, through experiencing the power of unity, worship and teaching that they step out in faith and give their lives to Christ.

Regardless of how it happens, we want to be part of it. We are missional, we are attractional. We are all things to all people, because we love the world like He loves the world!

13: The Living Room

Bringing people beyond the front door is the biggest challenge for conventional and emerging churches alike, whether stemming from a failure to help people transition to the "Living Room" or whether there simply isn't a living room in place.

It's not enough to just get visitors to church. We need to help them get plugged into the Body of Christ.

We want the welcome and accessibility that people experience at the front door to act as more than an entry point, but as a point of momentum. We want there to be a flow *towards* the living room, where people begin to feel at home and get closer to making a solid and permanent commitment to moving in.

We treat this the same way we would if we invited a person into our home. We wouldn't invite someone to our home and then never let them past the foyer. The same truth applies to churches—even more so. You've heard people call their church a "family" and that is ultimately what we strive for at CenterPoint. Family members do not arrive at the front door and then stay there. They come in and hang out in the living room with you. They make themselves at home, so much so that they eat the last of your Lucky Charms, especially the marshmallows!

So, What is the Living Room?

You could say that within our "House" concept, the living room is any place where people begin exploring what it means to become a committed member of the church. It is any program or event where people are no longer passive attendees, but active participants.

Sunday is a part of the living room to a degree, especially for those who serve on a Sunday. Our goal however, is to make sure that Sunday is not the peak of a person's living room experience.

People can plug in to a variety of living room experiences. Here are a couple of the primary avenues:

Life Groups

These small group meetings, ironically enough, often take place in folk's living rooms. Whether at someone's home, at the church building or office, some Life Groups are Bible studies and others are discussion groups. Some are prayer groups and others address a particular need or topic. Each Life Group, no matter what the topic, is marked by truth, grace and fellowship.

It is our hope that Life Groups become one of the primary ways that people get connected to others, find healthy, nurturing and caring relationships, grow in Christ and find accountability. Our hope is that a deeper sense of community is born in Life Groups.

Volunteer

One of the best ways to help someone get connected in a church, is to help them find a place to serve and use their gifts. We are always looking to create more opportunities for people to serve at CenterPoint. We have many needs in our church from making sure bagels and coffee are available to greeting folks and handing them bulletins on Sundays. Others may be more interested in helping out with building and maintenance needs. Still others might want to help by serving the homeless or visiting patients in the hospital.

We've seen people really hit their stride in a living room context by rising to the occasion when disaster struck—for example, when our basement flooded three times in the spring of 2010! I never thought destruction could be a good thing, but people who had never been plugged in at CenterPoint before became committed family members after a few weeks of shop vacs and demolition.

We're excited to say that many more living room experiences are developing at CenterPoint. In addition to the "regular" weekly and seasonal ministries, we make sure that a variety of activities are available so people can connect. We have events on our calendar such as "Beach and Baptism Day," a rafting and tubing trip, and an outing to a Minor League Baseball game. If a church doesn't play together, well then, it's just boring! Having fun is also a goal in the living room.

Whether it is through working, playing, gathering, sharing or learning together, you see: *The underlying theme of "living room ministry" is to help people plant roots within the church and build relationships with others in an environment where they can grow together in Christ.*

And this underlying theme is important so that:

- We get to know one another and feel safe.
- We see solid examples of Christian living.

- We begin to recognize a person who has been marked by Jesus.

- We realize that this Christian community matters and that it can make a difference in our own lives.

When these things begin taking shape, we begin the final step of "Moving In."

14: Moving In

A person who has "moved in" has officially become a member of CenterPoint. But don't let the technicality of membership take away from what's really going on: When someone moves in he or she is fully engaged in the life of CenterPoint Church, and beyond that, is personally committed to helping fulfill its vision in our community and world.

Our members own the vision for themselves and know that not only are they *a part of* CenterPoint, but they *are* the church.

Someone who has moved in is marked by three distinct characteristics:

- A continual pursuit of God.

- A biblical stewardship of resources that the church needs to accomplish its vision (i.e. time, talents, spiritual gifts, finances and so on).

- Missional living (bringing the church to others).

It is our great joy when someone officially partners with us. With so many people checking out our church, it's often hard to know who are the people of CenterPoint. Becoming a member lets the church body know without question—this is your church.

BEYOND THE VISIBLE

We know that no metaphor can fully capture the spectrum of personality types, nor how each person responds to a church community. So even as we have listed some characteristics of a person in the moving-in stage, we recognize that some folks do all these, but still haven't taken root in the church. They have trouble going beyond the exterior and into the intricacies of church life. While it may be easy to get involved in programs and volunteer, to live missionally and even to give time, money and energy, some find the openness and vulnerability of moving in an insurmountable obstacle. They cannot let down their guard enough to trust others, and perhaps even God, and consider what it means to be a part of a church "family."

What stinks is that someone can go on like this for a

long time, doing what it takes to be a part, but never really feeling connected.

For those of you who recognize this in yourself, please know that we understand.

There is vulnerability involved with being a fully committed part of a community. Risk is inherent in love, in giving, in serving and also in sharing and sacrificing.

But you are not alone! We are all a work in progress, and moving in is a process. If you are pursuing God, praying for His power in your life and desiring to do what Jesus would do, God isn't through with you yet.

It takes both a seed and soil for a plant to grow. When we move in, we encounter dozens of gardeners that work in the fields alongside us. This is why we move in.

Living for Christ is an organic process and, as the Bible says, produces an abundant life. This doesn't mean that we spend all our time dancing in fields and that life is happy and scot-free. It means that in the ups and downs, the defeats and victories, the struggles and the momentum, we have Him, each other and a long-lasting harvest in which to share.

At CenterPoint, we desire to reflect the life of God before the people in our communities and all of Long Island. And then, hopefully, to draw them into His house!

Part 4:

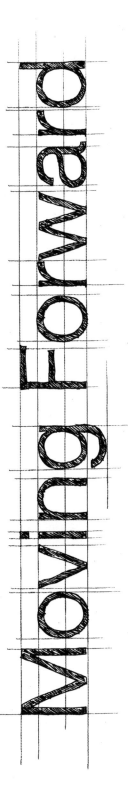

Moving Forward

15: Chapter One

NOT FORGETTING THE GOAL

I hope that in this book I have captured the heart of CenterPoint, simply put, to show people Jesus. This is our desire, plain and simple. We are missional and we are attractional. We teach Christ and we strive to emulate Him. Our church structure encourages people to walk through the doors and to engage in the ongoing conversation about God. We take steps so they can move into authentic fellowship and see the church at work in their lives.

In so many ways, this isn't the final chapter of *Design*, but the beginning of a much larger story.

The purpose of *Design* is to explain our approach in reaching people for Christ. We haven't discussed so many other vital aspects of what it takes to be a spiritually healthy church. This can include raising up leaders, church government, true spiritual formation, humanitarian outreach and equipping our members in their own callings.

Reaching people with the Gospel isn't the end goal, it's only the beginning. We want people to know God's call on their lives, beginning from the first step of knowing Jesus as their Savior through the ongoing process of making Jesus their Lord as well.

The conclusion of this book isn't the end of our philosophy on ministry. Our work is far from over!

WARNING

I often wonder if Christian books, churches and seminaries should come with a spiritual warning label. WARNING: *The theology or philosophy taught here, when combined with certain personality traits or attitudes, could be misleading or even dangerous.*

Even if something starts for the right reasons, it can still have destructive consequences if it goes astray. This happens when we lose a Biblical balance and run to extremes. Countless times in the history of the church, the spiritual pendulum has swung back and then forth. A simple thought that once sparked revival becomes dogma or, worse, blatant sin.

Even our attempt to reach people for Christ can become a stumbling block for the church! This is something I realized as I taught a series at CenterPoint called "Killer-ism's." We discussed the destruction of certain "ism" topics such as legalism, individualism, materialism and consumerism. As I prayed about the message on materialism and consumerism, I wondered how much of these ideas have crept into the church. Though my message was a practical one about financial responsibility and finding contentment in Christ rather than "toys" and name brands, it made me think: If being a consumer has become such an intricate part of our society, and possessions often dictate our self-worth, this must also be affecting the way we conduct church.

Even after the series ended, these questions remained at the forefront of my mind. I started to wonder if, in our focus on drawing people to know Jesus as their Savior, have we been faithful to show them how to make Jesus their Lord? Did we play on their consumerist tendencies in order to get them in the doors and come to Christ without ever showing them the next steps of faith?

The Apostle Paul says in Philippians 3:8, *"What is more, I consider everything a loss because of the surpassing worth of knowing Christ Jesus my Lord, for whose sake I have lost all things. I consider them garbage, that I may gain Christ."*

How many of us would consider the things we value most in this world, "garbage" compared to knowing and serving Jesus? The more we progress in our faith, the more we put aside "the things of this world" in order to gain more of Christ.

We need balance in the Church: If we pour all of our energy into reaching people, then all we will do is create Christian consumers.

Now don't burn this book too quickly! Before you wonder why I just brought you through fifteen chapters only to contradict myself in the end, think about this: How did we come to faith? We were all "consumers" when we first came to Christ. We discovered that Jesus was the answer to our main problem: We needed forgiveness. We needed His love and salvation. It was all about us.

The very morning I realized just how lost I was, I put my faith in Christ. I didn't like my lifestyle. I didn't like who I was becoming. I had made so many mistakes. I felt like a failure. And in my brokenness, I cried out to God to forgive me and make me new. I needed Jesus.

We come to Jesus because of our spiritual needs. And through this step of faith, Jesus becomes our Savior.

But God's call on the church isn't just to show people how to "get saved." We are called to teach people how to make Je-

sus the Lord of their lives. This is the process of making disciples.
Jesus couldn't have made this more clear than He did in
His last words to His disciples:

> *"All authority in heaven and on earth has been given*
> *to me. Therefore go and make disciples of all nations,*
> *baptizing them in the name of the Father and of the*
> *Son and of the Holy Spirit, and teaching them to obey*
> *everything I have commanded you. And surely I am*
> *with you always, to the very end of the age."* (Mat-
> thew 28:18-20)

Did you catch that? Go and make *disciples*.

The word "disciple" has strange connotations in these
modern times. We don't have a proper context for it. In fact, today the word is often associated with religious uprisings or cults.
I think the word scares us a little. But "disciple" was commonly
used in Jesus' day. In fact, the first Christians were called disciples.
It says in Acts 11:26 that the *disciples* were first called Christians
at Antioch. If you were a Christian, you were a disciple of Christ.

Remember my recommended warning label for Chris-
tian literature? Take heed even with this book: Though we believe
in the importance of having a strong focus on reaching people,
taken to an extreme, *attractional qualities* tend to become *consum-
eristic.*

Don't be so attractional as a church, that you forget to teach Christians what it means to be disciples. If you don't make disciples of the people in your church, you only perpetuate the instinctive consumer within them. That is unhealthy, and it's unbiblical.

CHRIST FOR SALE

Let's get personal for a moment. If you are an American Christian you are probably, to some extent, a Christian consumer. Before I get ahead of myself, allow me to confess: "Hi, my name is Brian. And I am a consumer."

I struggle with this as well. When I want something, I want it my way, on my timetable and as conveniently as possible. Preferably with one click and before anyone else can get it.

Have you heard stories about those pathetic consumers who stand for days outside an Apple store whenever a new iGadget launches waiting for something they think will add meaning to their lives? They stand on line with a cheesy grin that announces, "Yes, I'm a dork." Sad. Yet I am one of them and have spent far too much time on lines waiting for my own iDevices!

I am a product of my culture. And this culture invades the church.

Material items aren't bad, buying them isn't inherently evil. Our economy is based on buying and selling. However, when this becomes something we expect from Christ and His church, then it becomes an issue.

Jesus didn't have a problem drawing crowds. He was actually great at it. Some people came to see his miracles. Others came to be dazzled by His intellect and hear His sermons. Some just came because of the hype, and since they didn't have TV yet, I'm sure listening to Jesus was more enjoyable then weaving another basket at home. All Jesus would have to do is start teaching in the middle of an open field and, before you knew it, thousands of people would be there listening to Him.

But Jesus' goal wasn't to build crowds. His goal was to speak into the lives of just a few. Twelve in fact. These twelve guys followed Jesus everywhere and called Him master. These twelve learned the definition of "disciple" as set by Christ. So when Jesus told them to go and make disciples, they knew exactly what He was saying.

In Matthew 16:21-23, Jesus explains what it means to be a disciple:

> *"Jesus began to explain to his disciples that he must go to Jerusalem and suffer many things at the hands of the elders, the chief priests and the teachers of the law, and that he must be killed and on the third day be raised to life. Peter took him aside and began to rebuke*

him. 'Never, Lord!' he said. 'This shall never happen to you!' Jesus turned and said to Peter, 'Get behind me, Satan! You are a stumbling block to me; you do not have in mind the concerns of God, but merely human concerns.'"

No doubt, this hurt and embarrassed Peter. Jesus verbally attacked him. He called him Satan! But what Peter wanted to see Jesus accomplish wasn't what He was called to do. Peter wanted Jesus to assume a position of worldly power, a physical kingdom. But Jesus came to become Lord of the heart, not Lord of the land.

Then Jesus said something shocking to His disciples: *"Whoever wants to be my disciple must deny themselves and take up their cross and follow me. For whoever wants to save their life will lose it, but whoever loses their life for me will find it."* (Matthew 16:24-25)

If I had been in that little group of disciples, this would probably have pushed me over the edge. Carry my cross? You have got to be kidding me. Did Jesus even know what He was saying?

Remember, the cross, to a Roman citizen, symbolized shame! It was far from becoming the piece of beautiful jewelry that it is today. No one would choose to receive a cross. The cross meant death. It was an execution device that was excruciatingly painful and publicly humiliating. Yet Jesus said in order to follow Him, you must carry your cross.

That is exactly what Jesus did for us.

And that is what He calls us to do for Him. A true disciple of Christ denies his own desires, takes up his cross and follows the desires God has for him, not his own.

It is hard for us to recognize all the areas in our lives in which we are consumers rather than disciples. Most of the decisions we make tend to revolve around *self*, even if we don't realize it.

What do I want?

How does this make me feel?

What do I get from this?

Yet a disciple removes "self" as the priority. On the Mount of Olives, knowing that the cross was before Him, Jesus prayed to the Father, "Not my will, but yours be done." This should be our prayer as well.

Just how prominent is consumerism within the church? Here are a few comparisons of a "Christian Consumer" versus "Christian Disciple:"

CHRISTIAN CONSUMER	DISCIPLE OF CHRIST
• Is happy with Jesus, as long as He's convenient	• Puts Jesus as the center of life, no matter what
• Wonders what they can get from Jesus?	•Asks what can they can give to Jesus?
• Will run away when things get hard	• Understands trials and persecution are part of life
• Hears about Jesus when a pastor teaches	• Walks with Jesus daily
• Believes stepping out in faith is for others	• Sees living by faith as a daily exercise
• Sees their time, money, skills and talents as their own	• Sees everything they have as God's gift and wants to use it for the kingdom of God
• Never mentions their faith	• Their faith is seen and heard by those around them
• Reads only the parts of the Bible they agree with	• The entire Bible is the authority of their life
• Doesn't commit to one church body, but uses multiple churches' programs	• Finds one church where they commit and serve
• Looks for a church based on a shopping list of programs	• Looks for a church based on prayer and seeking a place to serve

Don't scribble in other people's names next to certain categories! This list is not meant to be ammunition by which to judge others, but for ourselves to take stock of our own attitudes toward our faith.

Jesus is not a commodity! The Church should not be in the "business" of selling Jesus. The Church is here to make disciples of Jesus.

I'm convinced that the distinction between consumer and disciple is a battle for the heart of the Church, for God's people. The Church will fade into oblivion if we as Christians don't change our perspective from consumers to disciples.

As we continue to be creative in reaching people for Christ, as we try to be all things to all people, we must remember this: The Church needs to set the example of paying the price of following Christ. We must show people how to move from accepting Jesus as Savior to making Him their Lord.

Final Thoughts

This last chapter could easily be the first one of a new book. Any good movie always sets itself up for the sequel, right? We would eventually like to examine the intentional process of discipleship and we at CenterPoint are fully diving into that process. I hope you are as well.

Design is not just about our church, but about our pursuit of God and finding our voice as a church. It is about a journey of discovery that all Christians are making. Our destinations may vary greatly, but our goals should be the same. This is our story of listening to God, hearing His call and following His design.

Notes

CHAPTER 1:

Matthew 28:18

John 1:1-5, 12-13

CHAPTER 2:

Matthew 17:1-5

CHAPTER 3:

1 Corinthians 1:27

CHAPTER 6:

2 Corinthians 5:17

CHAPTER 7:

Luke 10:38-42

Exodus 33:12-18

Romans 12:1

CHAPTER 8:

The Shaping of Things to Come, by Michael Frost and Alan Hirsch. Copyright © 2003 by Michael Frost and Alan Hirsch.

CHAPTER 9:

A New Kind of Christian: A Tale of Two Friends on a Spiritual Journey, by Brian D. McLaren. Copyright © 2001 by Brian D. McLaren, Jossey-Bass Inc. Reprinted with permission of John Wiley & Sons, Inc.

CHAPTER 12:

The Poisenwood Bible, by Barbara Kingsolver. Copyright © 1998 by Barbara Kingsolver.

John 3:3

CHAPTER 15:

Philippians 3:8

Matthew 28:18-20

Matthew 16:21-25

Also from Brian McMillan

Hear more from Brian on CenterPoint's Podcast

on iTunes or at: www.cpchurch.com/messages